IN THE IMAGE OF God

Suwanee, Georgia

REV. PAUL A. MCFARLAND

In The Image of God
Copyright © 2012 Rev. Paul A. McFarland

All Rights Reserved.

No part of this publication may be reproduced, stored in a retrieval system, or transmitted in any form or by any means – electronic, mechanical, photocopying, recording, or otherwise - without the written permission of the author or publisher. The only exception is brief quotations in printed reviews.

First published by Faith Books & MORE
ISBN 978-0-9860159-0-8

Printed in the United States of America.

This book is printed on acid-free paper.

3255 Lawrenceville-Suwanee Rd.
Suite P250
Suwanee, GA 30024
publishing@faithbooksandmore.com
www.faithbooksandmore.com

DEDICATION

I delicate this book to my parents, Sylvanias and Juanita McFarland, who demonstrated real love and nurturing in my life and taught me to believe in myself, and also to my godmother, Joanne (Big Mama) Turner who encouraged me in my youth and gave me spiritual guidance.

THANKS

I would like to thank the following: My wife, Mottie, who has tolerated my personality, and understood my purpose; my sister, Rochelle Howie, for her precious time in proofreading this work; and my dear friend, Valerie Price, who provided the typing services.

Foremost and all, I thank my God for this opportunity. He inspired me to start this project. I am grateful to the First Salem Baptist Family. I also would like to thank Faith Books & MORE Publishing for its assistance.

chapter ONE

THE IMAGE

THE IMAGE

Each day when I wake, I give my God thanks for I realize it is by His grace and mercy that I am able to inhale and exhale. Through His power, I can use these limbs. Some may take these blessings for granted or have no idea how blessed they are for life as it is. Nevertheless, whether or not we realize it, we all have good reason to praise God for His goodness toward us! The book of Genesis 1:31 records: "And God saw everything that He had made, and, behold, it was very good." It is pleasing to hear the approval of God in what He created.

God had an idea. What was this idea? A society; a community of being. This was created not because He was lonely, for there were all the residents of Heaven that are the Angels. This idea was formed from nothing and made into something that no man or scientist can explain: First, the creation of the universe, then the creation of living creatures, then the ultimate—man. And not just a man, but a man in His own image. This image was of power, of wisdom, of knowledge, a man of intelligence able to learn and understand the divine purpose and the will of his creator, "God."

The book of Isaiah 43:7 teaches us that man was created for God, not God for man. And yet though man was made for God's pleasure, man can find pleasure in Him—God. This is a divine pleasure.

From the beginning man and woman have been pleasure seekers; seeking that certain something to fill that void, that dark hole, that emptiness which in all cases affects their lives emotionally. It seems that man still searches for that which satisfies the desires of his flesh and that which gives him a sense of security. Therefore, man's existence became a burden and he cannot be in the image of Him who created all things and said, "It is very good."

We have in some form adopted, not the image of God, but a corporate image. I am saying that we are burdened in trying to become acceptable to this manmade concept of how man shall live. This is what burdens us. We feel the need to live up to man's standards, and once these standards are met in our lives, we have joy. This is misleading because maintaining a position that man has decreed for us calls for much labor, and with all this labor comes hardship, malpractice, dishonesty, wrongdoing, and infidelity. Could this be the yoke Moses spoke about in the book of Deuteronomy 28:48: "Therefore shall you serve your enemies which the Lord shall send against you, in hunger, and in thirst, and in nakedness, and in want of all things: and he shall put a yoke of iron on your neck, until he have destroyed you"? Because this is, what is going on in our lives, as we turn from God's standard to follow man's standard. Our God says in Matthew 11:29-30 that if we live by His standards it will be easier and lighter for us to bear.

I don't want to contradict myself when I say that God blesses the child who has much because God intended that man should have much (see Genesis 1:27-31.) The real question is, did God give it to him or did he take it? There are those who do not have God in their lives and yet they have much and are laboring hard to hold onto what they have. This means doing anything they have to do to keep it. And when I think about the system that this society operates by, it does not leave me wondering.

God's image for man is to walk in His perfectness. And once in His perfectness, we are rich. However, until we get beyond the standard of material possessions as success that has been established by society we are no longer in the image of God. To be in God's image is to project what is on the inside—love, care, piety, compassion, mercy, forgiveness, understanding. These are what man lacks.

I have learned that whatever man sets out to seek, he will find. The reason we do not find it sooner is that we look for it in the wrong ways. I say "ways" because we are blind in a world of darkness. Only when we seek the Lord first can we receive the light to see in the darkness of this world.

Jesus, our God, says in Matthew 6:33 (KJV): "Seek ye first the Kingdom of God and his Righteousness, and all these things shall be added unto you." Now the question is, how do we seek the Kingdom of God? This has been asked of me many times. My answer is to meditate on the living Word of God and live according to the precepts of Jesus Christ, which are godliness. This is a Godly image. Once we learn the will of God and understand it to the fullest then we must exercise it in our daily lives. This is the Kingdom of God—that perfect society God intended from the beginning of His creation.

Too many times, I meet people of all races who are searching for something to fulfill their lives. I, too, once was this person. If I did not have money, cars, girls, or great material possessions, I felt less than someone who had all these things. This kind of attitude contributes to what society has set up for mankind as standards. Then when I psychologically prostituted myself to meet man's standards and achieved what was conceived to be success, I realized there was yet a void—still an emptiness—in my life.

At some time and point in our lives there should be a fulfillment, a completion, a sense of satisfaction. How, then, can one be satisfied if he/she labors so hard to gain and keep what is only temporary? Too much emphasis is put on a material life and too little on a spiritual life.

Isn't the will of God that we be perfect as He is (Matthew 5:48)? Therefore, perfection is not based on what we have, but on who we are if we are in the image of God. In order for one to be in the image of God, one needs to know that without faith life cannot be enjoyed to the fullest that God has for whosoever. However, with faith in God one can be satisfied with life. With all God's promises and attributes, we lack nothing.

David says in Psalm 23:1, "The Lord is my Shepherd, I shall not want." This is good to know; that God provides for all of our needs. This is the substance of life; to be in tune with God. To be in tune with God is to have faith in Him, and to have faith in Him is to believe in Him, and to believe in Him is to lean on Him.

As I mentioned earlier, when we search for fulfillment we tend to look in all the wrong places. Isaiah 55:8-9 teaches us where to find this fulfillment. In the gospel of John 14:6, Jesus says, "I am the way, the truth, and the life."

When God created man, He created a powerful being. When I use this term I mean a being able to think and act with inventive, logical concepts; to himself create. This does not make us equal to God, but it shows us that God has made us in His image and likeness, not only in the form of the body, but also in the psyche, the immortal part, the soul.

chapter TWO

A FALSE SOCIETY

The society we live in today is not that of God. We live in a world full of havoc. If we examine the circumstances of our society, we see that evil has disclosed itself. In addition, it plays a role in all our lives. It has an effect one way or another. We can look closely and see it in our political society, which directly, profoundly affects the economy that exists today. Not only has it left its mark on politics and the economy, but in homes as well because in our homes are practices of various forms of unrighteousness. This has led to thousands and thousands of divorces and abortions. This evil has also crept into our school systems. Therefore, as I stated, this cannot be the society God intended it to be.

I attended a Bible study one Wednesday night. The preacher was teaching the Covenant of God, the laws that were given to the nation of Israel. In his explanation, he failed to point out why these laws were given. Instead, he was more interested in how many times Moses went up and down the mountain. I was hoping he would use the political and spiritual implications that influence the reason for the Covenant of God.

If we note the book of Genesis, the first chapter informs us of the creation of the world by God. Its history tells us of His chosen people, of their bondage to their oppressors and their freedom from slavery. Then come the books of the Law (Exodus, Leviticus, Numbers and Deuteronomy). Here we plainly see that these people, God's chosen ones, did not have any form of government to govern themselves. Exodus 19:5 says: "Now therefore, if you will indeed obey my voice indeed, and keep my covenant, then you shall be a special treasure unto me above all people: for all the earth is mine." If God's people would obey His voice and keep His law or Covenant, they would be a gem in His eyes.

Not only do I profess Jesus, but desire Him also. Because of my deep feelings about my calling to Christ, I can say that God will make you special to Him. That is not to say you are not already special to Him, because He did create you and I, but those who have elected to follow and obey Him are a treasure in his sight!

My calling is proclaiming the Word of God to God's people in the African American Community. I have seen that most people refuse to submit their lives to God's will. This bothers me, because to accept Jesus is to be governed by God's Commandments. However, I received a revelation that has become a theory for all this disobedience.

My theory goes back to the history of Black Slavery as well as the Word of God. When one examines Black history in these United States, we learn about the pain and suffering that has been inflicted by the oppressors. This idea of being owned by a Master who told us how, when, and where to live and punished us for not following orders, which sometimes led to death, left a remembering in the back of our minds that some will never forget.

There were people who were possessed with such evil that they inflicted so much hardship and discrimination. This history started the Civil Rights Movement led by Rev. Dr. Martin L. King, Rosa Parks and many more. We think about how long our ancestors suffered vicariously for us.

Now let us go back to the term "master." A master is one who rules others or has control, meaning to have power over someone or something. When the word master pops up a psychosis takes shape, which can have a psychological effect. In other words, certain things we hear and receive can trigger our minds for good or bad, and I believe when we hear the word "master" or Lord, it triggers what I call the "slave man mentality" and results in negative actions and images. That is why disobedience occurs so often in the lives of God's creation.

Once again, I am saying this is my theory concerning why human beings are not always obeying God's word. Biblically, disobedience is to rebel against recognized authority. Second Samuel 16:19-21 illustrates this idea of rebellion against authority.

In order to walk in the Image of God, we must obey Him. Psalm 37:23 says: "The steps of a good man are ordered by the Lord." This means if a man wants this godly image, he must let God have total control over his life.

The society we live in now is not the one God intended for His creation. For man has, by his influence, created a society suitable for man and governed by man's laws. The Bible teaches us to respect even the laws established by man, but God did not create this type of society for His people. In the book of Romans 10:1-3, Paul says, "Brethren my heart's desire and prayer to God for Israel is that they may be saved. For I bear them witness that they have a zeal for God, but not according to knowledge. For they are being ignorant of God's righteousness, and seeking to establish their own righteousness, have not submitted to the righteousness of God."

I believe this is the reason there is so much confusion in

today's society. We have witnessed the injustice that exists. It has caused bitterness, sorrow, and pain in our lives and caused us to experience the hurt from unfair practices. Man may have exploited us, but to be in God's Image we must learn to endure much of this hardship. Those that experience this fashion of life are normally the poor and of low income—those who suffer the handicap of living in poverty, the ones who have not been given their fair chance—those that have been rejected by society and looked down on because of the economic disadvantages in their lives.

This brings up the idea of two societies that man has created: the very rich and the very poor. We know that the voice of the poor goes unheard. This was true ever since what is known as the inter-testament period in Biblical time when the rich and elite separated themselves from the lower classes because there was no middle class. Today, there is still no middle class. Man would have us believe there is, but in reality, the middle class is equal to the lower class.

In the eyes of the wealthy, the poor are the ill favored those who are in need. We are not going to go into why they are poor, but we can establish the fact that in essence, the poor have existed from the beginning of time. Our Lord Jesus says in Matthew 26:11, "You have the poor always with you..." These are the people who are socially rejected. Is this not a form of segregation? Is this what God had in mind; to make two classes of creation pertaining to man, an upper class that is acceptable and a lower class that has no place on this God-given earth? I think not.

God has dealt with man from the very start, from the Old

Testament to the New. In addition, here in the New Testament we can see God deal with man in the flesh. God Himself corrects the problem that man has made for himself—God in Jesus or Jesus in God. A new idea is given to man on how to live, a conceptual difference that would make man better.

Jesus came so that man might live a life of joy. He came to reestablish a new world order. God made a new and better Covenant that supersedes the old one because we have found flaws in the old Covenant. This is not to say God made a mistake, because God is too wise to make mistakes, but he seems to think that man needs a second chance. This old Covenant dealt with the laws of the Old Testament and did not give man a second chance in life, but the new Covenant does.

In viewing the action that is taken by God, it can very well be said that man needs to overlook his standard that we have erected for society to live by. If one reads Hebrews 8:7-13 one could see and feel God's compassion. Jesus teaches us how to live a different lifestyle. He gives us the idea in His "Sermon on the Mount" in the book of Matthew, chapters 5-6. What Jesus is doing is creating a new society, a counter-culture community. Our religion is based on the imagery that society has produced for us by man's idea. This is far from what God would have us practice. Rather than being what man says we ought to be, God created us to be like Him.

Therefore, I ask this unfair question: Who is more superior, man who was made a little lower than the Angels or God who created the Angels and all else? How can we be so blind to the fact that God is our creator who directs our path whether it is peace or war, life or death? Do we control our own lives? Can we not consider the ultimate power that is beyond our reach?

The disposition in which we find ourselves can lead to many hardships that go unanswered. I think we need to disassociate from the standards man has created and take on the standards God created for us in the beginning of time. This is not to rebel against the laws of the Lord, but to transform into the Image of God, to personally accept his ideals and ways as to how man is to live.

Once I believed that with all the suffering and pain in my life, life was unfair. The unhappiness and misfortune that seemed to be regularity had left me to think that was just the hand I was dealt. Yes, it was the hand I was dealt, but not from God—from man. I was trying unsuccessfully to live up to man's standard and not God's. When I was exposed to the light in John 8:12, where Jesus said, "I am the Light of the world," then I realized how long I had been in darkness. That revised my thoughts and feelings.

To be in darkness has two effects. One is psychological, dealing with the mental state, and the other is spiritual, dealing with moral aspects.

Let us look at the psychological point. To be in this darkness is to not easily understand the whys of life. In addition, that which is not understood can affect one's disposition. This darkness brings a sort of coldness to one's attitude because darkness is associated with cold. When the mind perceives something as unjust or unfair, it triggers an emotional state that results in disorienting behavior. Children rebel against parents when they think they are being treated differently than other siblings of the same family. Hardworking employees can have this kind of behavior when they perceive that they are not being treated the same as others. A wife or husband can have the same disposition from feeling this psychological darkness. This can have a profound effect in one's life.

In King Solomon's quest for joy and happiness, he realized they could be obtained in life for only a short time. Therefore, he was able to establish the fact that to the one who seeks satisfaction based on philosophy or science and not God, life will be full of human problems and complexities. It will be a life of vanity.

We must realize that the uncertainties of life and the certainty of death show that God's purpose and ways often cannot be grasped. One should magnify the opportunities while they last because fortune can change suddenly.

I believe we can lose a great deal of time on a dream and hope that is beyond our reach. So it seems that we should certainly take every opportunity to seek the will of God. Isaiah 55:6 says, "Seek the Lord while He may be found. Call upon him while He is near."

So besides God, what is it that man searches so hard for? Is it fame, riches, security, happiness? Whatever it is, it is promoted out of self-satisfaction. As we continue to explore our existence and expediently look to our findings, to that level of man's standards, then we realize, as Solomon did, that it has all come to be vanity.

These years that have been given to us for the sole purpose of worshiping and glorifying God have been wasted. Now time has become somewhat against us. As we have become old and bitter, our bodies become feeble and frail. The mind now plays an unstable role. We cannot think and reason as necessary. Men and Women everywhere have wasted precious time seeking the things of this world. Only when we study the theology of God can we understand that life has been predestined from the very beginning. We do not have time to waste.

In the book of Ecclesiastes, the King, "Solomon," lets us know from a divine revelation that "there is a time for everything under the heavens" (Ecclesiastes 3:1). God's purpose must not be confused with fatalism, a theory proved false by God's appeals to all men to repent and obey Him. We have learned early that Jesus created a counter culture community. Therefore, the theory known as Deism, that God is unconcerned about His world, is disproved by God's intervention in human affairs. Read Daniel 4:23-27 and John 3:16. They show us that God cares for His creation. The appeal to men and women that they should repent shows how much God does care.

To repent is a prescribed formula for the mind and heart of man. To repent is to change one's perception, actions, and behavior. This is what needs to be done in order to be in "God's" image.

I have seen in life that you can find happiness, joy, and security in Jesus Christ, only if you are willing to obey Him and keep His will.

chapter THREE

FIRST THINGS FIRST

The Apostle Paul, in his many letters to the Christian Churches, shows those people, as well as us, that to become recipients of life's blessing from God there is something we must do. First, we must separate ourselves from the world's standard of living.

This is where we fall short. We were created for a divine purpose, but our substance is based on the imagery of society, what man has made to be the standard. In this, there is no strong foundation to stand on. In the book of Second Corinthians, chapter 6, verse 17, the Lord says, "'Come out from among them and be ye separate,' saith the Lord."

Let us look at this word "separation." It is to set apart from others for a special purpose or become disconnected from others. Therefore, we will look at it from a divine revelation. Separation in scripture is twofold: (a) to be apart from whatever is contrary to the mind of God; and, (b) to be part of the will of God Himself. The underlying principle is that in a moral universe it is impossible for God to fully bless and use his children who are in a compromising situation with evil.

Now, let us see what it means to separate from evil. It implies the separation of desire, motive, and acts from the world. In the ethically bad sense, this present world system refers to the arrangement Satan has organized, the world of unbelieving mankind upon his cosmic principles of force, greed, selfishness, ambition, and pleasure. This world system is imposing and powerful with military might. It is often outwardly religious, scientific, cultured, and elegant, but seething with national and commercial rivalries and ambitions which are dominated by Satanic principles.

Separation is not from contact with evil in the world or in the church, but from complicity and conformity to it. The reward of separation is the full manifestation of divine fatherhood according to 2 Corinthians 6 verses 17-18. This is to say that this present world system would have all creation conform to its principles or standards that has been provided by man from the ruler of this world who is known as Satan. In addition, we do have the proof of this in the testament of Matthew's gospel in the fourth chapter, verses 8-9. Satan here is offering the world's riches to anyone willing to compromise the divine standard of God.

Therefore, we cannot give compliance, because what is our compensation for this act? Are we to labor so hard for a reward that is death? Paul informs us in Romans 6:23 "that the wages of sin is death but the gift of God is eternal life through Jesus Christ, our Lord." Paul also found out that the commandment that was ordained to life was unto death.

"And God said, 'Let us make man in our image after our likeness'" (Genesis 1:26). Man was created, not evolved. This is expressly declared and Christ in Matthew 19 confirms the declaration: 4. The fact that God, at the beginning, made them male and female confirms the declaration.

It is also confirmed by the unbridgeable gap between man and beast. The highest beast has no God-consciousness, which is a form of religious nature. Man was made in the "image and likeness" of God. This image is found chiefly in the fact that man is a personal, rational, and moral being. While God is infinite and man finite, nevertheless man possesses the elements of the personality similar to those of the Divine creator God in thinking, feeling, and willing.

That man has a moral nature is implicit in the record and is further attested to by the New Testament in the book of Ephesians 4:23-24 and Colossians 3:10. Man is also the image and glory of God according to First Corinthians 12:7.

Just as we see the Trinity of God in the persons of FATHER, SON, AND HOLY SPIRIT, there is also the Trinity of man—body, soul and spirit. Because "God is a Spirit", we must worship Him in spirit and in truth. This tripartite nature of man is not to be confused with the original "image and likeness" of God which, being spiritual, relates to the elements of his personality.

Though God gave man dominion over the earth, yet he is subject to God, his creator. The divine intention was and is that man should have fellowship with God in obedience. So why is it so complicated to be in His image if He has created us in His image?

This question is not hard to answer. The reason we choose not to be in His image is because sin interferes, creeps up, and man yields to it, which causes a divine separation between God and His creation, man. This was the sin of the first man, Adam, and all born after him were born in sin. In addition, because of this act of sin and disobedience, God handed down the ultimate sentence—death to the body and soul of man. If man repents and gives his life back to his creator, who is God, and accepts His standard for the life He intended, and then man can live a life of joy and fulfillment.

This is the reason for the Gospel of Jesus Christ—that we may receive salvation from God. Man, for this purpose, needs an example, a sort of model to pattern after. If we can conform to a society that is not of God, once learning the truth about God's will, we can emulate Jesus' life.

How often have we heard these words: "I am not perfect"? This cannot be true if we were created in the image of God. Perfection in one sense means completion. Therefore, if we have the personality of God—the mind to think, feel, and will as God does—can't we feel as perfect as He does? Yes, we can be perfect. I believe this because Jesus confirmed it in the gospel of Matthew 5:48: "Be ye therefore perfect, even as your Father, who is in heaven, is perfect." This perfectness of God is not based on His creation, but is a manifestation of His character, which is an expression of purity, honesty, and charity.

This is the image of God, and it is by this imitation of life that the Christian counter-culture becomes visible. Too often, this statement, "Be ye perfect," has been misinterpreted. It has served as a basic text for the doctrine of what is known as Christian perfectionism, which requires of the Christian absolute moral impeccability. However, that often ends up reclassifying sin as something less than it is. Therefore, the perfection to which Jesus calls the world as well as His followers has just been defined by the context.

Perfect love is an active concern for all people everywhere, regardless of whether or not they receive it. Therefore, to do this is to imitate God and demonstrate that we are His children, His creation, and His offspring. In addition, when we act out this role in our lives it is a display of family likeness.

The Greek word "teleios" (perfect) means, "having attained the end/purpose." Since human beings were made in the image of God, they are "perfect" when they demonstrate in their lives those characteristics that reflect the nature of God. Once again, Paul gives us a clear picture of God's purpose for us in Romans 8:29. It says, "For whom He did foreknow He also did predestinate to be conformed to the image of His son, that He might be the first born among man brethren." The Apostle, having reckoned up so many ingredients of happiness of true believers, came here to represent the ground of them all, which He lays in predestination. This is to say that life for man has always been planned by God's divine blueprint for life. This is the love of God for His creation, that through Jesus, His image, we may be conformed to it.

Now this problem of darkness has crept into this life from the prince of this world, Satan, who has blinded us from seeing the true purpose of God's, will. That will is to be in His image, to live the life of Godliness. This concept to be in His image is real for man who was created by the hand of God—that not only is man to be perfect in a world that is dissipated, but to be prepared for this soul of man. Therefore, I come to learn that man can find happiness in God, to know God had to be God in his spirit, that man can be successful without seeking the things of this world.

Jesus asks what profit a man has if he gains in the world and loses his only soul. Therefore, to gain is wasteful for a man who does not know the will of God. To gain that which will perish is vanity for man. The flesh of man must return to that from which it was created. The spirit has no need for that which pleases the flesh of man because the spirit of God's creation will not find itself dwelling on this God-made earth. It dwells in that which God has prepared for it, heaven or hell. We then must continue to seek the will of God until the return of Jesus and do that which is expected of his creation, to resist evil and draw near to Him (God), to love and care for one another, to pray for all, to show mercy toward others, and to be just in our judgment, not bewildered in our efforts to find the joy that man has placed as the priority in one's life.

In my conclusion, there is only one precedent in one's life—that is God, who is first. When we acknowledge this fact—that God is first and everything else comes not in front of Him but behind Him—only then can we experience the blessing of God that will bring the joy we seek so diligently. To exhibit this feeling from the love of God will reassure us that one day we can abound in the Grace of God. This is the "Image of God." This peace surpasses all understanding.

Our quest is not for the things of this world that will give us happiness, but to submit to the will of God, which will please Him. This, then, can show our faith in God. We must totally rely on the wisdom of God to keep us in perfect harmony with His divine plan. Our faith must be in God. We must trust in the words of Jesus Christ if we are to draw close to God.

If only we can realize how much God has to offer us in his divineness to make our lives full and rich with His joy and success in His completeness, because without Him we cannot be complete. We cannot receive that joy.

Jesus says in the gospel of John 15:5, "Without me you can do nothing." Learning this should show us that all we do is through the grace of God. His love through His son Jesus shows us how much He loved us, even to the point of giving up His only son, Jesus, so that we might have life beyond this earthly point.

God must be first in our lives each day. He needs to order our steps for He has created them. We need to lean on Him, for He is our strength; He is the hope of our tomorrow and the trial of our yesterday, which He has safely brought us through. Without Him we cannot be all we would like to be, and that is not the image man would have us believe in.

You must believe in the power of God to bring about your miracle. Write this down. It is not enough simply to want a miracle to occur. You must also believe that the miracle can manifest by the power of God working through you.

How any times have you heard it said: "With God all things are possible"? What does that mean to you? Is it just a worn-out slogan that has lost its magic? Something on the order of, "Have a nice day"? Well, think again! Give it back the meaning it had when Jesus first said, "With men this is impossible; but with God all things are possible" (Matt. 19:26). In other words, you cannot do it, whatever "it" is, by yourself. Your humanness is not strong enough. You must balance yourself out. You are spirit, soul, and body.

Perhaps you have had, or now have, negative restricting emotional habits. The fact that you have had these habits is no reason they must be with you always. Desire a change. Believe God can bring it about then begin working the law and you will see yourself changing so beautifully that you will probably say, "Wow! Look from where I came. Look where I am!" and "Thank God I have somewhere to go!"

Once in the image of God who has created all things, one can receive this blessing. The power that is within each of us is unspeakable and yet real. This is where faith kicks in—to only believe in Him and yourself that all things are possible in Christ. This does work. From my own dealings, I have found that God is the way for those who trust Him and His will.

Let us remember that God has given us laws for all mankind to live by. If we will govern ourselves by them accordingly, then we are walking by faith and not by sight. This is what pleases God. When our walk pleases God then we can receive the blessing from the Lord. Only then can we find happiness apart from this world if we believe in Christ.

Let us look at Romans 8:28-29 (KJV). This will confirm that God had a plan for his creation. "And we know that all things work together for good to them that love God, to them who are the called according to his purpose. For whom He did foreknow, He also did predestinate to be conformed to the image of His Son, that He might be the firstborn among many brethren." Holiness consists in our conformity to the image of Christ.

This takes in the whole of sanctification. Christ is the express image of his Father, and the Saints are conformed to the image of Christ. Thus, it is that we have God's love restored to us and God's likeness renewed upon us. How divine it is to be restored back to the love of God! How blessed we are to have a caring God, who is willing to be there to see us through, who is the light in our darkness!

"Amazing Grace how sweet the sound, that saved a wretch like me. I once was lost, but now am found, was blind but now I see." This is my testimony, as well as the testimony of millions and millions of others. Until we come to the light, we cannot experience God's Grace that gives a new meaning for life, a life in Christ. There can be success in life, completeness, self-satisfaction, if your life is in the image of God.

To start changing to this new image we need instructions and the only instructions can be found in the Word of the Lord. Proverbs 4:7 says, "Wisdom is the principal thing: therefore get wisdom; and with all your getting, get understanding."

chapter FOUR

THE POWER TO CHANGE

In the book of Romans 12:2 (AMP) the apostle Paul writes, "Do not be conformed to this world, (this age), [fashioned after and adapted to it's external, superficial customs], but be transformed (changed) by the [entire] renewal of your mind [by its new ideals and it's new attitude], so that you may prove [for yourselves] what is the good and acceptable and perfect will of God..." Paul informed his readers that through Christ we have a divine power to change our lives.

There is a combination of spiritual and psychological influences that enable individuals to take control of their destinies and gives them power to change their circumstances. This power is given unto mankind from a supreme being.

As I mentioned earlier, we were created in the image of the almighty God; therefore, there is given to us a measure of power that lays dormant within us all. If it were in any way possible to obtain the DNA or the fingerprint of God and that of man and to put them under the cosmic microscope of existence, there would be evidence of the strands that would determine that there is a hereditary characteristic between God and man, the connection between the creator and His creation.

We see in the book of Genesis 1:26, "God said, 'Let us make man in our image, after our likeness.'" In the gospel of John, Jesus said also, "I and my Father are one" (John 10:30). This profound statement implies that the power of God dwelt within Jesus; therefore, He had the authority to assure His followers that He was able to provide for them that elected to follow Him. However, one must understand that changes produce responsibility.

This is where what appears to be a difficulty begins. Most people welcome a change in their circumstances—in their finances, their relationships, their careers, their appearance, where they live, their friends, their lifestyles—yet most are fearful of changes in their lives. For the most part changes are good. It has been said, it a poor wind that never changes direction or course!

Again, Paul said, "Be transformed by the renewing of your mind" (Romans 12:2). To transform is to change the nature, function, and condition of the state of mind and behavior of an individual. There are situations in life that can cause you to desire a change because of the bitter taste that comes with being yoked in a society of disadvantage and being victimized and mistreated by the principles, deeds, and actions of corporate American. We find ourselves in desperate need of change.

There were times in my life when my spiritual blindness led me into a pool of despair and sorrow. I was drowning in my own self-pride and ignorance. In addition, when I came to myself, as the prodigal son did, after spending immeasurable time in the hog pen of life, I realized there must be a change in my circumstances. I made changes in my life for the better, or else I would have been lost in the hog pen forever, an unpleasant disposition.

I am responsible for my actions. Therefore, I have realized that in order for me to change my situation I had to begin by eradicate the negative image of my life and start focusing on a positive one. I had to surrender my self-will, adopt, and embrace the will of God. I understood that I must give Him (God) absolute control of my being. Once He had control then

I was endowed with power to change.

Jesus said, "I am the way, the truth, and the life, no one come to the Father except through me" (John 14:6). We must establish a relationship with Jesus the Christ in order to have a connection to God.

I have heard that when a couple stays together for a period of time they begin to look alike, think alike, act alike, and often talk alike. We are to emulate the characteristics of Jesus by acting, talking, and thinking just like Him. Then we will begin to look like Him in the eyes of God.

There is a sense of completeness when you can achieve your spiritual goal. This is one of the stages of maturing in Christ—to know that there is a purpose for your life. There are some who have not yet discovered their true purpose, and they are still wandering in the wilderness of deception, fooled by society, misled by propaganda and empty promises birthed in this world by none other than the great deceiver himself (Satan).

God can—and does—give us the power to change our lives, our circumstances, and the environment we occupy. He gives this power so that we are able to challenge our sense of logic that causes us sometimes to miss the mark. A power I am speaking of is the power of the Holy Spirit, or the Holy Ghost of God. Once we understand the purpose of the Spirit of God, we can expeditiously receive this power from God, because his purpose is to empower the believer of God to do all things in the name of Jesus.

Praise God, I am feeling it as I am writing! In Roman 8:37,

Paul informed his readers, "Nay, in all these things we are more than Conquerors through Him (God) that loved us." Matthew 3:16 (KJV) records, "For God so loved the world, that He gave His only begotten Son, that whosoever believeth in Him should not perish, but have everlasting life."

This is the power to have victory in your life, to overcome the obstacles that are before you, to claim or take your destiny and the promises of God. So if connected to Christ Jesus, we do have the power; the power to change our lives, the power to affect those around us, the power to direct our destinies, the power to reach our goals, the power to manage our affairs, the power to think and to reason, the power to defeat our fears.

Isaiah 26:3 says, "You (God) will keep him in perfect peace, whose mind is stayed on you." Your enemy, the devil, would have you feel insignificant as well as miserable, lacking self-esteem and confidence in your ability to achieve. Therefore, once the mind is clear of those things that have no purpose in your life except to hinder your progress and discourage you, you have the power to change your circumstances.

In Luke 24:49, Jesus said, "Behold, I send the promise of my Father (God) upon you; but tarry (wait) you in the city of Jerusalem, until you are endued with Power from on high." The Bible lets us know that God will supply all of our needs. Only through the power of God can a person change their lives.

Job was a man of affliction who had lost everything he owned—his livelihood, his children, his wife—and his friends who could not understand what he was going through abandoned him. You will also encounter people who will not understand what you are suffering or what you are going through. However, Job had power within. He was connected to a divine source, which was God. Job said, "All the days of my appointed time will I wait, till my change come" (Job 14:14). If changes are to come, there must be a process for these changes to develop. Job's soul did not change, but his mind and environment did.

It is imperative at times through the process of changing that our minds develop as well as our environments. There are times we must remove ourselves from certain situations and environments. Though transformation brings about a change, sometimes that change consists of how we view our situations. This is actually the process that demonstrates the development and maturity of an individual.

Nothing should remain the same forever. If I surround myself with a negative environment, I will become like or adapt to that environment. That is why it is very important to investigate and take assessment of my life. If I am to move forward, I must take a retrospect of my life as to where I am. Only then can I make the necessary approach to begin the process for change.

Therefore, before I can change the environment I am in, a change first has to occur inside me. I believe this is what the Apostle Paul meant when he spoke of "the renewing of the mind." This is where change begins—in the mind, heart, and soul of a person.

In my early years as a pastor, I was led to believe that emphasis on the structure of the church was more important than establishing a solid relationship with God. A nice building was more desirable than anything else was. Then I begin to witness the deterioration of the spiritual being within God's children, as they became a dysfunctional body of Christ because of the lack of a proper spiritual diet. They were suffering from spiritual malnutrition.

If there is a disability in your life that is preventing you from tapping into the divine source of empowerment to change your life and overcome the obstacles before you, you must examine your situation. Acknowledge your weakness and open your mind to the renewing that comes from the Word of God. The Word of God will not only renew your mind, but also activate the power within and give you the strength to change. There needs to be a connection between God and you through Christ Jesus to receive the power of God.

chapter FIVE

THE WILDERNESS EXPERIENCE

Exodus 16:4: "Then said the Lord unto Moses, 'Behold, I will rain bread from heaven for you, and the people shall go out and gather a certain portion every day, that I may prove (test) them, whether they will walk in my law, or not.'"

Whether or not we are aware of it, we all have wilderness experiences in our lives. They are a measurement of our endurance and perseverance, a test of will and submission.

When we have not yet discovered our purpose in life there are times when life becomes our wilderness because we have no stability. The book of Romans 12:3 says, "God has dealt to every man the measure of faith." This word "faith" can easily refer to the talent of an individual, one's abilities or aptitudes, quickness in learning and understanding, the ability to think in a time of urgency, to discover one's purpose, the meaning of existence, and how to contribute to it. When we find purpose, we then obtain stability and a sense of direction.

Everyone needs to know where he or she came from and where he or she is headed in life. We need to know our past and present in order to take the proper steps toward our future. We must learn and understand how we arrived where we are and what it will take to get where we are supposed to be in Christ.

Sometimes because of refusal to follow directions and instructions, we begin the journey of wandering in the wilderness, a place of confusion and isolation. There will be signs of deception and misdirection.

Because of refusal to follow divine direction, the children of Israel found out their forty-day journey turned into a forty-year quest in search of the promise of God. Sometimes the promised blessings of God can be finger's length away, but if we refuse to submit ourselves to the will of God and to follow divine instructions from the Word of God they become unreachable.

The book of Proverbs 3:6 says, "In all your ways acknowledge Him (the Lord), and He shall direct your paths." When we submit to God's ways and will, allowing Him to order our steps, we learn that the path he prepared for us is an easy one to follow if we do not allow ourselves to be distracted.

You will learn on this journey as you strive toward your destiny that there will be lessons learned when you encounter them. In addition, each obstacle you come face to face with will be no more than a stepping-stone toward your purpose and the promises from the Lord. It is your faith in God that will empower you to overcome the obstacles in your life. You must trust in the Lord and depend on Him to get where He wants you to be.

God tested the children of Israel. Would they be obedience to His commands and submit themselves to His directions or would they be influenced according to the flesh by what they could see?

If you are to be great, you have to learn to trust in God and in His everlasting Word. The book of First Chronicles 4:10 speaks of a man named Jabez. He prayed to the God of Israel saying, "Oh that you would bless indeed, and enlarge my border, and that your hand might be with me, and that you would keep me from evil, that it may not grieve me!" Because of Jabez's faith and willingness to follow the directions and instructions of God, God granted him that which he requested. "He (God) is a rewarder of those that diligently seek Him" (Hebrews 11:6).

If you can learn to trust God for everything you need He will grant you your requests. I can say that I have received everything I have desired in my heart because of my willingness to follow the direction of the Lord. Even things I never thought I would receive God made possible for me to obtain. In addition, right now, if He does not bless me anymore for the rest of my life, He has done more than enough for me.

The wilderness I speak of has no geographical boundaries. Whenever we are out of the will of God we put ourselves in a wilderness situation—a place of desolation, wandering in the void and emptiness of life, misdirected, with no sense of purpose. Only when we submit ourselves to the will of God can we come out of our wilderness.

God wants man to explore all the possibilities He has prepared for human consumption. In the book of First Corinthians 2:9 we read, "But as it is written, Eye has not seen, nor ear heard, neither have entered into the heart of man, the things which God has prepared for them that love him."

If God is leading you in the wilderness, He is still with you. In addition, if He walks with you in the wilderness, He will see you through it. However, as you make the transition from the wilderness to the purpose and promises of God, you will experience pain, suffering, and loneliness. Your faith in God will be on trial and your principles will be scrutinized.

If we make the best of our wilderness experiences we can all enjoy what the Lord has prepared for us, but we must stay focused on the Lord. He gives perfect peace to those whose minds are stayed on Him. Therefore, we can endure even the wilderness experiences, the valleys, the mountains, and the widest rivers.

God will see us through our difficult times. As bad as this economy might appear right now, the Lord will prepare a table before you in the presence of your enemies. God is still making a way out of no way. Jesus said in John 14:1 "Let not your heart be troubled; you believe in God, believe also in me." What a word of comfort and encouragement! All I have to do is believe in God and His only begotten Son Jesus. There can be no room in life to entertain doubt about the infinite power and wisdom of God's abilities.

Now here it is: how to become the image of God. In order to grow in Christ, as you begin your wilderness experience, there must be a period of devotion and consecration. When you come to your lowest point of life, that is the time to seek the Lord without interruption and to meditate on His divine Word. Being in the wilderness allows you opportunity to come into the presence of God that you might begin to establish the relationship that is needed to know the ways and will of God. You might say, "How can I start a relationship in the mist of my personal crisis?"

Your crisis allows you the motivation to pray, search, and meditate on Him as well as to re-evaluate the mistakes you have made. The Bible says to seek the Lord while he may be found, and sometimes you cannot find him if you allow the distractions of self-will to come between you. They will prevent you from knowing God's will.

How many times have you promised to read your Bible or to attend Bible studies? How many times have you said to yourself, "I am going to Sunday school next week," and six months pass you by? You must rebuke the spirit of complacency and take back control of your destiny. You must come to the reality and understanding that God have something good waiting for you. In addition, you cannot allow anything to get in your way!

Brothers and sisters, I am excited about your future! May the God I serve and worship bless you richly.

www.ingramcontent.com/pod-product-compliance
Lightning Source LLC
LaVergne TN
LVHW051205080426
835508LV00021B/2809